Lake District

oviding a wonderful panorama of water, fell and mountain, the Lake District National Park
ompasses almost 900 square miles of the most diverse scenery in Britain. Bustling market towns
ntrast with the solitude of lonely upland tarns and ancient forests. Placid lakes are overshadowed by
ijestic mountains which rise sheer from the waterside, while racing streams and tumbling cataracts
ead the landscape. Here are to be found both England's highest mountain, Scafell Pike, and its largest
e, Windermere. No two sheets of water are the same. Windermere and Ullswater are popular for all
ms of water pursuits, while on others like Wastwater, England's deepest lake, and remote and
spoiled Ennerdale Water, private craft are prohibited. White-washed farmhouses dot the landscape,
d in towns and villages old buildings cluster in quaint corners. Lakeland provides a rich habitat for
dlife including the graceful little roe deer and the mighty red deer. Among the birds which can be
n, buzzards are common and golden eagles have returned after an absence of 200 years. .

Wordsworth's Lakeland

Acknowledged as one of the greatest English poets, William Wordsworth is closely connected with the Lake District where he lived for many years. Born at Cockermouth in 1770, he attended Hawkshead Grammar School and eventually settled at **Dove Cottage**, *right,* in Grasmere. With his sister Dorothy, he moved into this simple whitewashed cottage in 1799. It was here that he brought his bride after his marriage in 1802 and they moved from the cottage reluctantly in 1808 when their family outgrew it. It was while living at Dove Cottage that the poet wrote many of his finest poems. Today the cottage is maintained as a museum to his life and work. **Rydal Mount**, *below,* in the village of Rydal was Wordsworth's home from 1813 until his death in 1850. The house, which contains many portraits and mementoes of the poet's life, is situated in beautiful terraced gardens which Wordsworth himself designed and created.

The area around Ullswater was greatly admired by Wordsworth whose famous poem *The Daffodils* was inspired by the sight of wild daffodils growing in profusion at **Gowbarrow Park**, *above*, on the northern shores of the lake. Wordsworth himself planted a spectacular mass of daffodils on the grassy slope adjacent to Rydal Mount which was named **Dora's Field**, *below*, after the poet's much loved daughter.

On his walks Wordsworth would keep a record of the people and places that he saw, drawing on them in his work and creating a picture of life in 19th century Lakeland which is as accurate as that of any social historian. Together with his sister, his wife and three of his children, Wordsworth is buried in the churchyard of St. Oswald's Church at Grasmere.

Grasmere and Rydal

Enfolded in a typically beautiful Cumbrian landscape between Ambleside and Grasmere, lovely **Rydal Water** is the smallest sheet of water in the Lake District to be designated a lake. Surrounded by trees which somewhat obscure it from the road, it is best seen from the footpaths which circle the lake. Rydal Water is owned by The National Trust which controls the use of boats on the lake, thus helping to preserve its peaceful atmosphere.

One of the prettiest of the lakes, **Grasmere** is enclosed by steep fells which rise up from the wooded shores. There are many attractive walks around this placid lake, and rowing-boats can be hired to visit the small wooded island. The village of Grasmere nestles at the foot of the hills on the far side of the lake which was a constant source of inspiration to Wordsworth.

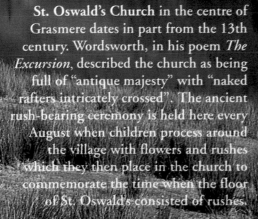

St. Oswald's Church in the centre of Grasmere dates in part from the 13th century. Wordsworth, in his poem *The Excursion*, described the church as being full of "antique majesty" with "naked rafters intricately crossed". The ancient rush-bearing ceremony is held here every August when children process around the village with flowers and rushes which they then place in the church to commemorate the time when the floor of St. Oswald's consisted of rushes.

Around Ambleside

The attractive market town of **Ambleside**, *main picture,* is situated on the lower edge of Wansfell at the northern tip of Lake Windermere. It is a popular base for visitors to this part of the Lake District and is busy for much of the year with tourists, walkers and mountaineers. Ambleside received its first charter in 1650 and consequently it possesses many attractive old buildings which date from this prosperous period in the town's history. The centre of Ambleside has been designated a conservation area and among the interesting buildings which are preserved is the quaint 17th century **Bridge House**, *left.* Spanning the little Stock Ghyll, it was originally built as a summer-house for the orchard of Ambleside Hall and is now used by The National Trust as an information centre.

The road from Ambleside to Coniston passes through the hamlet of Skelwith Bridge in the beautiful Brathay Valley. Close by is the picturesque waterfall known as **Skelwith Force** *left,* where the River Brathay and the Langdale Beck combine and tumble over a sixteen-foot drop.

Situated between Red Screes and Caudale Moor, the **Kirkstone Pass**, *right,* carries the main road from Ambleside to Patterdale. A wild and desolate area, this is the highest pass in the region open to motorists, reaching 1,489 feet near the Kirkstone Pass Inn. From the summit there are magnificent views of the surrounding area with the fells sweeping majestically down towards Patterdale and the little tarn known as Brothers Water.

Stock Ghyll is a delightful little mountain beck which rises on Rcd Screes and flows south through the centre of Ambleside. Just outside the town is **Stock Ghyll Force**, *left*, a fine waterfall where the water tumbles down a rocky glen overhung with trees and ferns, dropping a total distance of some seventy feet.

Ancient **Jesus Church**, *below,* at Troutbeck was rebuilt in the 1730s, and a major restoration which took place in 1861 included some superb glasswork by Edward Burne-Jones, William Morris and Ford Madox Brown. The church-yard is notable for its yew trees, its three lych gates, and the war memorial cross which consists of a single slab of Lakeland stone.

Around Windermere

The most southerly and, at ten miles long, the largest of the lakes, **Windermere** lies in a valley formed by glaciers during the Ice Age. The head of the lake is bordered by wooded slopes and lush fields. As the most accessible stretch of water in the Lake District, it is popular with sailing enthusiasts, and passenger steamers have operated on the lake for 150 years. Facing west across the lake, **Bowness-on-Windermere**, *above,* has been in existence since Viking times and is now well established as a resort and boating centre. The Royal Windermere Yacht Club has its headquarters here and Bowness Bay is one of the ports of call for the steamers which call regularly at the pier-studded waterfront to carry passengers the length of the lake.

Adjoining Ambleside at the north-eastern corner of Windermere, **Waterhead**, *right,* is a popular holiday and residential area. A good starting point for walks in the magnificent scenery of the Lake District, it is primarily a busy centre for boating activities of all kinds and another regular port of call for steamers.

The Lakeside and Haverthwaitc Railway was originally a branch line of the Furness Railway which carried passengers and freight from Lakeside to Ulverston and Barrow, then south to Lancashire. This was closed by British Rail in the 1960s, and now all that remains is the 3.5 miles from Haverthwaite, through Newby Bridge to the terminus at Lakeside. From April to October restored steam trains offer a passenger service on this steeply graded railway which passes through beautiful Lakeland scenery beside the River Leven in the Leven Valley. At Lakeside on Windermere the railway connects with the lake steamers. *Cumbria*, a locomotive which was built in 1953, is one of a number of former industrial locomotives working on this line.

Set in a tranquil lakeside setting, the **Windermere Steamboat Museum** houses a unique and historic collection of boats which reflect the nautical heritage of the Lake District. Many of these have been lovingly restored after lying neglected and derelict for years. The earliest of these, a yacht named *Margaret*, dates from 1780 and was discovered in use as a hen house. Other exhibits include the oldest mechanically powered boat in the world, a steam launch raised from the bed of Ullswater in 1962, and the rowing boat which belonged to Beatrix Potter, author of the famous *Peter Rabbit* books. A special exhibition relating to the *Swallows and Amazons* stories of Arthur Ransome includes the steam yacht *Espérance*, which provided the inspiration for Captain Flint's houseboat, as well as the original *Amazon*.

Around Coniston

Halfway between Coniston and Windermere, situated near the head of Esthwaite Water is **Hawkshead**, *right,* a Lake District village of great charm and character. Here there are many quaint old corners where stone cottages cluster in secluded courtyards, their cobbled pavements colourful with flowers. The Parish Church of St. Michael stands above the village overlooking the Esthwaite valley. The present building dates mainly from the 16th century, but the first church on this site was built in Norman times by the monks of Furness Abbey.

Between Hawkshead and Yewdale to the north-east of Coniston is the open wilderness of **Tarn Hows**, *below,* an area of wooded fell country surrounding a pretty little tarn. Now a single sheet of water, this was once three tiny lakes until a dam was built which joined them together. Tarn Hows is considered one of the prettiest of all the lakes and tarns, and the tiny islands and rocky promontories which jut out into the water from its wooded shores add to the beauty of the scene. This pine-fringed beauty spot is part of a vast estate once owned by Beatrix Potter, author of *Peter Rabbit* and other nursery classics, who became a respected Lakeland farmer and landowner. Her home, **Hill Top Farm**, *left,* at Sawrey, is now owned by The National Trust, and the 17th century house is a place of pilgrimage for thousands of visitors each year. The delightful cottage garden, with its rich profusion of flowering plants, features in several of her books.

With its wooded banks and pretty little islands, **Coniston Water**, *above,* is one of the most beautiful lakes and Coniston village is a popular centre for exploring this part of the Lake District. From the north-western shore of the lake, the distinctive peak of the Old Man of Coniston, pitted with old mine workings, rises from the water's edge to a height of 2,635 feet, offering panoramic views. First launched in 1859, the Steam Yacht *Gondola* plied across Coniston Water until 1937. After many years of neglect during which she was buffeted by storms and rotted on the lake bed, she was rescued by The National Trust and restored to her original Victorian elegance. Now returned to service she again carries passengers in opulent surroundings and offers a leisurely way to enjoy Coniston's beautiful scenery.

The largest forest within the Lake District, **Grizedale Forest Park**, *below,* is situated between Coniston Water and Windermere. Within the forest there are waymarked walks, cycle routes and a sculpture trail. The sculptures, created by a variety of artists in many different forms, are scattered around the forest amongst the trees, in woodland glades and alongside the paths.

The Langdales

Part of the High Raise group of mountains, the dramatic **Langdale Pikes** tower over the Great Langdale Valley. Although there are many higher peaks in the Lake District, the distinctive shape of the 2,300 feet high Langdales makes them a well-known landmark. The ascent rewards climbers with magnificent mountain scenery and views down into the valley, which is a popular centre for exploring some of the Lake District's most appealing beauty spots.

A tiny sheet of water almost encircled by trees, **Loughrigg Tarn** lies to the north of Skelwith Bridge beneath the slopes of Loughrigg Fell. There is an easy footpath along the wooded shores from which the distinctive, jagged shapes of the Langdale Pikes can be clearly seen.

In an attempt to establish their own supremacy, the Romans were the first to drive a road across the fells at the time of the Emperor Hadrian. Stretching from Kendal over the Wrynose and Hardknott passes to the sea, it effectively divided the power base of the local tribes. A chain of forts was established along the road to house the soldiers who were based here. At **Hardknott Fort**, which commands unsurpassed views of Eskdale and the Scafell mountain range, the remains of extensive Roman buildings can be seen including the bath house, granary and barrack blocks.

On top of a ridge above the Little Langdale Valley north of the Wrynose Pass, the shining deep blue waters of remote **Blea Tarn**, *main picture,* are cradled by steep fells. With its banks densely covered with fir trees and rhododendrons, and the surrounding landscape dominated by the jagged peaks of the impressive Langdale Pikes, it makes a perfect subject for artists and photographers.

The **Little Langdale Valley**, although it lacks the grandeur of neighbouring Great Langdale Valley, nevertheless provides good walks and some superb scenery. Picturesque Slater's Bridge spans the River Brathay as it runs on its way towards Elterwater, where there are quarries still producing the fine green slate which is a traditional local building material.

Western Lakes

Stretching for some seven miles between impressive mountains, Ennerdale is one of the longest as well as one of the most remote valleys in Lakeland. **Ennerdale Water**, *left,* with its heavily wooded banks, is overshadowed by a number of impressive mountains including Pillar. One of the highest peaks in the Lake District at 2,927 feet, it provides a challenging climb, but the view from the top amply repays the effort.

Situated two hundred feet above sea-level in the midst of Wasdale's forbidding but beautiful landscape, **Wastwater**, *right,* is the deepest of all the lakes, plunging to a depth of two hundred and sixty-eight feet. Rising up from the shores of Wastwater near Wasdale Head is Great Gable, one of the highest peaks in the Lake District. Chosen as the emblem of the Lake District National Park, the view of Great Gable and Wastwater is typical of the dramatic Lakeland scenery. The jagged, snow-covered peak of **Scafell**, *below,* which also rises high above Wastwater, is popular with climbers. It is one of only a handful of English peaks reaching a height of more than 3,000 feet.

Immortalised in a sequence of sonnets by William Wordsworth, the **Duddon Valley**, or **Dunnerdale**, *above,* is one of the more lonely and secluded valleys in the Lake District. The rocky and fast-flowing river rises near the Wrynose Pass and flows for ten miles to the sea. Northwards along the coast is **Whitehaven**, *left,* once the third largest port in Britain. It still has a small fishing fleet and its harbour has been declared a conservation area. The Beacon, on West Strand, contains displays on the town's history as well as a weather station.

The Ravenglass and Eskdale Railway is England's oldest narrow guage railway, built in 1875 to transport iron ore from Eskdale to the coast at Ravenglass. It operated on and off until 1960, carrying both freight and passengers. Now, one of the Lake District's most popular tourist attractions, it is run by a Preservation Society and provides a spectacular seven-mile-ride through Eskdale from the coast to the foot of the Lake District's western mountains.

Buttermere and Crummock Water

Although it is one of the smaller lakes **Buttermere**, *below,* which lies some 250 feet above sea-level, is nevertheless one of the more spectacular. It is ringed on three sides by steep mountains including impressive Hay Stacks. With its indented shore line and wooded slopes, **Crummock Water**, *right,* is one of the most beautiful of the lakes. Like most of the western lakes, it is surrounded by wild and romantic scenery, but the fells which enclose Crummock are less rugged than those in some other areas of the Lake District. A narrow strip of low-lying land separates Crummock Water

from Buttermere, to which it was at one time joined. From the summit of 2,791 feet high Grasmoor there are some of the finest views in the Lake District looking down on Buttermere, Crummock and Loweswater as well as the Scafell group of mountains. Originating as a small Lakeland chapel, the present **Church of St. Bartholomew**, *left,* at Loweswater mainly dates from 1884 when it was enlarged to meet the needs of the mining community.

Much of the scenery surrounding **Buttermere**, *above,* and Crummock Water is now owned and protected by The National Trust. Buttermere is a popular centre for exploring some of the wildest and most majestic scenery in the Lake District. The massive bulk of Fleetwith Pike rises to a height of 2,126 feet from the southern shore of the lake.

On its way towards Crummock Water the little Scale Beck descends through a steep ravine surrounded by magnificent scenery. Accessible only on foot, **Scale Force**, *above,* where the water falls in dramatic cascades, is the longest fall in the Lake District, leaping one clear drop of 120 feet and having a total fall of 172 feet. Lying between the heights of Dale Head and Fleetwith Pike, the **Honister Pass**, *left,* provides access into Borrowdale. From the summit there are fine views of forbidding Honister Crag where the world-famous green slate is obtained.

Around Borrowdale

West of 2,560 feet high Glaramara in the
Borrowdale Fells, a little beck runs through
the Sty Head Pass and down alongside an
ancient pack-horse route towards Seathwaite.
On its way the track passes the fine waterfall
known as **Taylor Ghyll Force**, *right*.

Borrowdale is one of the most enchanting
valleys in the Lake District. It follows the
course of the River Derwent, enclosed by
wooded fells and towering crags which
conceal many delightful little dells and tarns.
The attractive village of **Grange-in-
Borrowdale**, *below*, was once owned by the
monks of Furness Abbey who kept a
granary, or grange, here. The village is
reached over an ancient, narrow, double-
arched stone bridge.

Described by Sir Hugh Walpole, who set his novel *Judith Paris* here, as "an exceedingly remote little valley", Watendlath, *above,* lies to the south-east of Derwentwater. The hamlet of Watendlath consists mainly of old farmhouses which have been bought by The National Trust to ensure that their traditional character will be preserved.

Situated on the lower slopes of Grange Fell, less than a mile from Grange Bridge, the remarkable **Bowder Stone**, *right,* stands precariously balanced on one end. This huge rock weighs 1,970 tons and is thought to have been carried from Scotland by glacial action. It measures 62 feet in length, 36 feet in height and has a circumference of 89 feet.

Keswick and Derwentwater

Surrounded by mountains and thickly-wooded fells, Derwentwater is known as the "Queen of the English Lakes". Much of its charm emanates from its rich blend of steep crags, feathery woods and tiny tree-clad islands. Rowing boats can be hired to explore the lake and, for walkers, well-defined footpaths circle the water, a distance of about twelve miles. **Ashness Bridge**, *right,* was probably built in the early 18th century and was originally used by pack-horses. The famous view from the bridge towards the lake is thought to be one of the best in the Lake District.

Standing on the banks of the River Greta beneath the slopes of Skiddaw, **Keswick**, *left,* is an attractive old market town with narrow streets and sturdy grey stone buildings. Among them is the Moot Hall which stands prominently in the market square.

The rocky, pine-clad promontory of **Friar's Crag**, *right,* near the stone-built market town of Keswick is one of the best-known landmarks in the Lake District. The critic John Ruskin described the view from the Crag as one of the three most beautiful scenes in Europe. It was from here in the 7th century that monks embarked to visit St. Herbert at his hermitage on an island on Derwentwater.

Tumbling through a ravine between the towering and perpendicular rocks of Gowder Crag and Shepherd's Crag, the stream falls in a cataract which is particularly impressive after heavy rain. **The Falls of Lodore**, *right,* were made famous in a poem by Robert Southey and from the Upper Falls there are fine views over Derwentwater.

The Northern Lakes

The oldest rock in the region – Skiddaw slate – is found in the northern Lake District where it was formed on the sea bed some 500 million years ago. It produces much smoother outlines than the rock created by volcanic action, but the peaks are nevertheless impressively high. **Skiddaw**, *right,* itself is the fourth highest mountain in England, rising to a majestic height of 3,053 feet above the town of Keswick where it provides a dramatic backdrop to both Derwentwater and Bassenthwaite. It is seen here across Calf Close Bay on Derwentwater. Most northerly of the lakes, **Bassenthwaite**, *below,* is separated only by an alluvial plane from Derwentwater to which it may once have been joined. Some sailing and canoeing are permitted on the lake, but priority is given to nature conservation.

In a strategic position on a hill to the east of Keswick stands the **Castlerigg Stone Circle**, *below,* one of a number of prehistoric standing stones which are scattered across the landscape of the Lake District. Although the origins of the circle are obscure, it is believed to date from about 1400 BC and may have been a Bronze Age meeting place used to monitor the progress of the seasons. It consists of some 40 stones in a large ring with a smaller group placed within it. The site was evidently chosen with care since there is a magnificent view from Castlerigg, unequalled from any other spot in the area, which encompasses most of Lakeland's highest and best-known peaks.

Little **Caldbeck**, *right,* to the north-east of Bassenthwaite, is an attractive Lakeland village with a pretty green and a duck pond. It is well known for its links with the legendary John Peel, hero of the famous hunting song. He died in 1854 and is buried in the churchyard of the ancient Church of St. Kentigern.

Founded in 1749 as a port on the Solway Firth for shipping coal and, later, iron-ore, **Maryport**, *left,* at one time also had a thriving shipbuilding industry. This seafaring heritage is celebrated in the Maritime Museum near the dock where steamships, a tug boat and other craft offer a taste of life on board ship. The harbour was once busy with trading vessels from all over the world, but today it is used mainly by sailing yachts and small fishing boats.

Full of character, the country market town of **Cockermouth**, *right,* is perhaps best known as the birthplace in 1770 of the poet William Wordsworth. The handsome Georgian house in which he spent his childhood is now open to the public and has been fully restored by The National Trust in the mid-18th century style.

Around Ullswater

Surrounded by some of the Lake District's most impressive scenery and picturesque beauty spots, seven-mile-long **Ullswater** is the second largest of the lakes. Dominated by impressive mountains, the head of Ullswater lies in a magnificently dramatic position. **Brothers Water**, *below*, its surface dotted with water-lilies, nestles at the foot of the steep descent from the Kirkstone Pass. Less than half a mile long by a quarter of a mile wide, it was named, according to legend, after two brothers drowned here.

A public steamer service operates from Glenridding Pier at the southern end of Ullswater. Calling at Howtown and Pooley Bridge, the elegant 19th century steamers provide a leisurely way of exploring the lake.

Pooley Bridge is situated at the northern tip of Ullswater in the midst of superb scenery. Iron Age remains can be found on the nearby hills and at one time Pooley Bridge itself was the setting for a large fish market held in the main square. Today it is a busy tourist village with hotels and guest houses. It is a popular centre for many outdoor activities including pony-trekking, fishing, sailing and, of course, walking.

One of the approaches to Helvellyn, third highest peak in the
Lake District at 3,118 feet, is along the famous **Striding Edge**,
above, a narrow path winding between two precipices. From the top
of the ridge, the little Red Tarn can be seen below and extensive
views across the Lake District and into Scotland are revealed. The
spectacular waterfall known as **Aira Force**, *right,* is situated near
Gowbarrow Fell on the north side of Ullswater. It plunges in a
sheer drop of 60 feet between precipitous walls of rock, and is
crossed by bridges which give dramatic views of the gorge and the
nearby rocky scenery. Numerous footpaths give walkers easy
access to the surrounding landscaped parkland and woodland.

Stretching for nearly four miles
Thirlmere, *left,* was created at
the end of the 19th century
when the valley was flooded to
form a reservoir. Two small
lakes were expanded and many
old buildings submerged,
including an inn where
Wordsworth and Coleridge
used to meet. A popular area
with walkers, there are many
footpaths and forest trails
through the coniferous
woodland around the lake.

eyond the remote Mardale valley lies
Haweswater, *below,* most isolated of all the lakes.
t was converted into a reservoir in the 1930s and
he village of Mardale lies hidden beneath its
urface. It is said that the bells of a submerged
hurch can still be heard ringing in rough
weather. Surrounded by steep fells and woods,
he lake provides a rich habitat for wildlife. Both
oe deer and red deer are found here and the
alley is one of the last remaining haunts of the
ed squirrel. Among bird life, buzzards,
parrowhawks, peregrine falcons and golden
agles all breed here and many smaller birds such
s warblers, redstarts and tree pipits are found in
he Naddle Forest on the eastern shores of the
ake. A circular walk around Haweswater winds
hrough the woods and beside the water.

Dalemain, *above,* near Penrith is a delightful
country house comprising medieval, Tudor
and Georgian styles. The fine gardens and
deer park, which are particularly impressive
in autumn, include a Tudor knot garden, a
Stuart terrace and a walled orchard.

Kendal

The prosperous and attractive town of **Kendal** is the main southern gateway to the lakes. It has many interesting old corners including Branthwaite Brow, with its typically Cumbrian slate-roofed, grey stone buildings, and the ruins of Norman Kendal Castle, birthplace of Katherine Parr who became the last, and surviving, wife of Henry VIII. The magnificent Town Hall is a testament to the importance of the town which was granted a market charter in 1189 and flourished on the wool trade from the 13th century.

Levens Hall south of Kendal boasts perhaps the most impressive topiary garden in the world. Created in the 1690s, it has been carefully maintained virtually unchanged for more than three hundred years. Rising up in the midst of the neatly hedged flower-beds are nearly one hundred clipped trees shaped into designs including gigantic chess pieces, peacocks and Queen Elizabeth I with her maids of honour.

Linked to the Troutbeck Valley by a steep and stony path which was once a pack-horse route, the peaceful **Kentmere Valley** stretches for about four miles. Overlooked by remote moorland and rugged crags, this is superb walking country which is particularly lovely when the trees are clothed in their autumn colours.